Red Gray and Blue

Frank A. Kaye

Order this book online at www.trafford.com
or email orders@trafford.com

Most Trafford titles are also available at major online book retailers.

© Copyright 2013 Frank A. Kaye.

All rights reserved. No part of this publication may be reproduced, stored in a retrieval system, or transmitted, in any form or by any means, electronic, mechanical, photocopying, recording, or otherwise, without the written prior permission of the author.

Printed in the United States of America.

ISBN: 978-1-4669-7255-1 (sc)
ISBN: 978-1-4669-7256-8 (hc)
ISBN: 978-1-4669-7257-5 (e)

Library of Congress Control Number: 2012923569

Trafford rev. 12/12/2012

www.trafford.com

North America & international
toll-free: 1 888 232 4444 (USA & Canada)
phone: 250 383 6864 ♦ fax: 812 355 4082

CONTENTS

Introduction ix

Analyzing the Ills of American Society 1

Are We Being Systematically Destroyed? 7

The Deterioration of Democracy,
    When Did It Begin? 13

Is America Going Socialist? 17

Why I Chose to Become an Independent 21

America, the Powerhouse 29

Why Are We Fighting a Twelve-Year War? 31

Commander in Chief, Why? 43

Another Voice from the Internet 49

Compilation 51

A Chapter for Our Veterans 63

Improving Quality of Life of Veterans 65

Veterans Need Some Answers 69

Veterans Need Better Reps 73

Letters to the Editor 79

Basic Solution to Our Budget Deficit	103
From the School of Common Sens-ology:	107
Look Who's Running the Show	115
Convention Time	119
Are You Mad Yet?	125
America Still the Greatest	131

To Princess Hohenzollern,

the love of my life for the past sixty-seven years.

Love ya, baby!

INTRODUCTION

MY PASSION FOR POLITICS BEGAN when I first took notice of the presidential bid by George Wallace in 1968 on the American Independent Party ticket. It intensified by closely following my hero, Ronald Reagan. Up until recently, I considered myself a Republican and a conservative. But as I mellow out with age, I look more closely on both sides of the big picture, and my perspective changes. Just so you know what you are about to read, let me explain the quirky color-coded title.

In this present-day lifestyle, we seem to label each other. Sometimes complimentary, sometime otherwise. We have a name for everyone. In this case, as often demonstrated on your TV screen, Blue represents the Republican Party—right, far right, left, far left, middle, conservative, ultraconservative, etc. Red stands for the Democrats—old Democrats, new Democrats, leftists, middle-of-the-road Democrats, secular-progressive kooks, liberals, ultraliberals, mostly just freeloading Democrats. You have already decided on my political leanings, haven't you? Not so fast, we'll get back to this later. And then there is the Gray, which represents the negotiating table that both parties shy away from. Since it takes the mix of black and white to make the color gray, perhaps black and white would be a better choice. However, I don't do the mixing.

The members from both parties are our representatives—elected by us, the people—and are the superbrainpowers usually coming from the legal profession, the business world, and even from the medical field. Lots of brain, no common sense. They love their thousand-dollar dress wear, their four-hundred-dollar haircuts, and each fights vigorously, not for what they really believe in or what their constituents tell them but for what the Washington lobbyists dictate and pay for. They never see eye to eye and rarely go to the gray area for dialogue where most problems can be resolved. Neither are they overly concerned with their primary obligation—*the constituents.*

For example, take the issue of abortion. Pro or con? If modern medical innovations indicate a seriously deformed fetus with little chance for survival, plus endangering the life of the patient, would this not favor an abortion?

On the other hand, when a perfectly normal child is predicted but unwanted, with adoptions being a popular alternative, then abortion could be banned. Each situation should be decided only by a certified board of medical professionals, preferably a board comprised of women. Now isn't there some room for discussion here?

Then there is the issue of gun control. You will never take away a patriot's right to bear arms. So don't mess with it. But there is room for dialogue. The right to bear arms does not give you a license to buy AK-47s by the dozen along with cannon or two. So gun control is needed. See how easy that was. The point that I am really trying to make is with all this so-called brainpower among these 545 leaders we, the people, send to Washington, there is lacking the very basic *common sense*.

Frank A. Kaye

So who am I? And why this book? I sincerely believe that the solutions to all major problems looking for resolve in Washington these days lie with the everyday, ordinary citizen, especially the older ones like me. You know—those of us they call the greatest generation, among other names. *Senior citizens*, that's not too bad. But *old fogeys*? *Old geezers* doesn't sit well with me. We move a little slower, our eyes and hearing are not the same, but I'll not admit to being over-the-hill. Don't count us out yet. Born in the twenties, we survived the depression of the thirties sans all the modern toys of the day—television, refrigerators, washing machines, dishwashers, computers. We attended and received our basic education from the grade school level where we learned the Pledge of Allegiance, the "Star-Spangled Banner," and "America the Beautiful." We learned of Patrick Henry and of his impassioned plea for revolution with his famous, much-quoted "Give Me Liberty or Give Me Death," and thus we became young patriots. Then we matured in time to participate in the greatest war ever fought for what we believed then and still do now is the greatest country in the world. Only now we are wondering what in hell is happening to it. Now, in the words of that famous American conservative Paul Harvey, here is the rest of my story.

At this stage, I began to wonder why I should even write this book. After all, what can I add to what has already been written by professional journalists and political pundits the likes of O'Reilly's *Culture Warrior*, Laura Ingraham's *Power to the People*, Dick Morris's *Outrage*, William J. Bennett's *The Death of Outrage*, and Zell Miller's *A Deficit of Decency*, among many others. In recent years, we learned of the scandalous lifestyle of the Kennedy family, the crooked regime of Richard Nixon, and the outrageous Clinton administration—considered the most corrupt and scandalous in our time. Yet we showed little outrage. What makes this generation so apathetic and seemingly uncaring? Nevertheless, despite what has been previously written, I will present my view—a view from the everyday-street environment and the opinions of the many veterans from all wars with whom I communicated with on a daily basis plus those of the e-mail world whose messages I value and am requested to pass on. Please continue.

ANALYZING THE ILLS OF AMERICAN SOCIETY

> I have lived, sir, a long time, and the longer I live, the more convincing proof I see of this truth, that; God governs in the affairs of men.
>
> —Benjamin Franklin

WE WILL NEVER SOLVE THE issues of our civil society unless we first establish once and for all and unequivocally the fact that America is a Christian nation and English is our official language. And further, remove the hyphen from Latin-American, Asian-American, Afro-American, plus all other hyphen-Americans and start to call ourselves all American!

Long before we declared our independence some 246 years ago, Christianity was evident. When Christopher Columbus first landed on our soil in 1492, his first act was to plant a cross in the sandy soil as a symbol of Christianity and to thank God for the safe voyage, he being a Catholic from Spain. His discovery brought many other explorers seeking opportunity and wealth to this newly discovered land. Among them was a German geographer who suggested that the newly opened part of the world be called America. Even the startled natives, whom the newcomers called Indians, would look up to the skies and chant to the unknown God for good weather to help their crops. America began as a God-loving, God-fearing, and God-worshiping people, and no one dare take that away from us.

Then came the pilgrims way back in 1620 who, upon escaping religious persecution, immediately gave thanks to the Almighty God in their Thanksgiving ceremonies. And ever since, God and Christianity are symbolized throughout the nation. As civilization moved forward in America, you'll note the strong belief in Christianity as evidenced by all the religious symbols displayed on all our government structures. On the building that houses the Supreme Court, you can see on the top of the building a row of the world's lawgivers, and each one is facing one in the middle who was facing forward with a full frontal view. It is Moses, and he is holding the Ten Commandments. As you enter the Supreme Courtroom, the two huge oak doors have the Ten Commandments engraved on each lower portion of each door. On the wall where the judges sit, you can see a display of the Ten Commandments. There are Bible verses etched in stone all over the federal buildings and monuments in Washington, DC, and did you know? James Madison, the fourth president and also known as the father of our Constitution, made the following statement: "We have staked the whole of our political institutions upon the capacity of mankind for self-government, upon the capacity of each and all of us to govern ourselves to control ourselves, to sustain ourselves according to the 10 Commandments of God," and did you know? Every session of Congress begins with a prayer by a paid preacher, whose salary has been paid by the taxpayer since 1777. Did you know? Fifty-two of the fifty-five founders of the Constitution were members of the established Orthodox churches in the colonies.

I have recently returned from a tour of Washington, DC. It was a tour sponsored by the Honor Flight Network, a wonderful organization whose mission is to fly America's veterans to Washington so that they may visit the memorials built and dedicated to their honor and their sacrifices in past wars. And it's all free. I learned for the first time in my life of *Laos Doe*. Do you know what it means? After learning of a detail never mentioned in Washington, that there can never be a building of greater height than the Washington Monument, I was also enlightened of some amazing historical information. On the aluminum cap atop the Washington Monument are two words: *Laos Doe*. No one can see the words. In fact, most of the visitors to the monument are totally unaware they exist, yet they have been there for many years. So what do those two words in Latin mean?

Very simply, they say "Praise be to God," further adding to my previous comments on America being a Christian nation. When the cornerstone of the Washington Monument was laid on July 4, 1848, deposited within were many items—including the Holy Bible presented by the Bible society. Praise be to God! Such was the discipline, the moral direction, and the spiritual mood given by the founder and first president of our unique democracy. "One nation under God." After reviewing these inspiring memorials and seeing how well they were planned and purposefully placed among all other historical structures surrounding the Capitol dome, I noticed with interest how the Washington Monument is visible from all angles, serving as the beacon. I returned home one proud American and couldn't help but think there must be some brains in this country after all. But where in the hell are they? How did these no-brainers get us into a $16 trillion deficit? Take a look, friends. That's the figure 16 with an awful lot of zeros behind it. I'm not sure I could deal with those figures. Nevertheless, I can't help but wonder, why? With the financial situation that we are in, why are we fighting what seems like a never-ending war with an enemy who operates out of tents and caves?

Now hear this: if fifty-seven countries can identify themselves as Muslims—even though they may be Syrians, Egyptians, Jordanians, Iraqis, Iranians, or whatever—and Israel, an independent country, can be recognized as Jewish both in nationality and religion and Spain and Portugal as Catholic, then once and for all, let us make clear to the rest of the world what this country was built on. America is a Christian nation, and we speak English. Like it or leave it. Once this becomes an undisputed issue, we can sweep off the table ridiculous topics like abortion, same-sex marriage, gays in the military, and other atheist beliefs. We can silence, once and forever, the small minority demanding the removal of God from our money, Pledge of Allegiance, and other traditional religious beliefs. It is with great regret and disappointment that America currently lacks the leadership of our founding fathers and lacks the courage to make this matter clear to the rest of the world. Not a living soul on earth today can deny the basic history of the birth of America or deny our American heritage. We are as stated in the pledge of allegiance, a nation under God. Let us keep it that way.

ARE WE BEING SYSTEMATICALLY DESTROYED?

THERE ARE SOME AMONG US that feel we are. However, if four years of Jimmy Carter did not destroy our nation, four years of Obamanation won't either. There is good and bad news on the subject. The bad news is the rapid pace at which the progressive liberals have made radical changes to our traditional democracy. These groups, up to now, have been somewhat successful in their efforts to remove God from all government grounds, restrict any form of prayer from public functions, and ban the recital of the Pledge of Allegiance, even banning the display of religious artifacts on government property, including crosses on veteran cemeteries.

The good news is, when you put our back against the wall, the fight only then begins. This radicalization of democracy has awakened the traditional patriots and sane Americans in the land. Prominent among those would be political pundit Glenn Beck as seen on the Fox News Network. I sometimes feel he has bugged my living room since his talk show expresses my exact sentiments. Due to our traditional apathetic attitude, the reversal to these radical changes may be a difficult one; however, the battle lines have been drawn.

Moreover, these are not the only changes that are taking place that affect our daily lifestyles. Of great concern should be the current administration in Washington that is leading us into a socialistic society. Am I the only one to take notice of this movement as stated in my previous book *What in Hell Is Going On*? There are those among us who proudly say this cannot happen to this great country. America will not let it happen. However, go ahead and maintain a do-nothing attitude, and you might wake up some morning living in a different world. Apathy is the greatest danger to our freedom. Radical changes of this nature should be the responsibility of our elected officials, people who we send to Washington as our representatives who up to now have failed America dismally. Corresponding with them is like whistling in the breeze. They are too busy disgracing themselves by their actions in perverted sex, lies, deceptions, and scandals. Sanford, Barry, Craig, Spitzer, Edwards, Ensign—these are but a few. There are many others. I don't know how factual this is, but this quiz has been circulated among the sports fans who were posed with the question. Is it the NBA (National Basketball Association) or the NFL (National Football League)? Thirty-six have been accused of spousal abuse, 7 have been arrested for fraud, 19 have been arrested for writing bad checks, 117 have directly or indirectly bankrupted at least two businesses, 3 have done time for assault, 71 cannot get a credit card due to bad credit, 14 have been arrested on drug-related charges, 8 have been arrested for shoplifting, 21 currently are defendants in lawsuits, and 84 have been arrested for drunk driving. Can you guess which organization it is? NFL or NBA? Neither. It's the 435 members of the US Congress, the same group that cranks out the laws that we, the citizens, have to live with. It is mind-boggling as to how we, the people, from every walk of life can be so indifferent as to vote into high political office the likes of a Jesse Ventura, former governor of Minnesota, an Al Franken to Congress, or an openly gay Barney Franks. And the latest to make the dirt list is Charlie Rangel, congressman from New York, whose constituents gave him a free hand, and he stuck it right into their pockets. Our country was in better condition when there were more whittlers and fewer chiselers. The United States Constitution is a great document with one defect: it does not require an intelligence test for congressional candidates. Do we not lose respect on the global level with this type of leadership? Voting in new faces periodically does not seem to solve the problems either. The system just seems dysfunctional.

Those of us who consider ourselves Christians, and I believe statistics show that to be a close 90 percent, can make a brief reference to the story of the tower of Babel, as written in the Bible, where men's attempt to build a tower with its top to reach the heavens was foiled when the Lord observed their ambitions and that they all spoke the same language. The Lord said, "If this is the beginning of what they will do, let us go down there and confuse their language so that they will not understand one another's speech." Not being able to understand one another, they scattered all over the earth. Do you think the Lord placed this same curse on our Congress?

Take a peek at the makeup and the demographics of our Congress, and tell me how it can work in unison. Out of 435 representatives sitting in office, there are 256 Democrats, 177 Republicans, and two vacant seats. There are seventy-five women, twenty-five Hispanics, forty-one Afro-Americans, nine Asian-Americans, two American Indians, and the bigmouth gay guy, Barney Franks. Is there a similarity to the men building the Babel Tower? Since there exists such a mixed conglomerate of legislators, do you really think this commingled bunch could forget their selfish needs and concentrate on the one goal of what is best for America? I don't think so.

Maybe we should follow this strategy for America's survival as was suggested to me by a fellow patriot: Since there are so many of us who believe that the entire Congress of the United States is corrupt, and I mean both houses and both major parties as a group of people (They are the most corrupt bunch to ever disgrace our nation. Never in the history of America have so few loused up so much for so many), why not clean house—both of them: the Senate and the House of Representatives?

Now the task remains. Where are we going to find 535 real, live, traditional American patriots the likes of George Washington, John Adams, or Thomas Jefferson? People who will put the interest of the country first. For when America is great, everything else will fall in line. Just about everybody will agree that our country is on the move, though there is plenty of argument about the direction. And remember, future candidates, in America, any boy can become president. We have one now.

THE DETERIORATION OF DEMOCRACY, WHEN DID IT BEGIN?

I'LL NOT PRETEND TO BE a scholar or a history buff, but ever since grade school, I have always taken a keen interest in the history of America, the beautiful. Maybe it was the often mention of Indians in our history books that did it. Boy, did I ever love those colorful Indians! I believe I was the only kid in a crowded movie theater showing a cowboy-and-Indian flick to root for the Indians. The point I am making here is my interests in history brings back fond and proud memories of the past and a reminder of our traditional values. You know—pilgrims, Plymouth Rock, Indians, trading, Thanksgiving, Fourth of July, church picnics, sandlot baseball, hot dogs, apple pie, Armistice Day parade, and a deep respect of moral values and love for thy neighbor—all that old-fashioned stuff.

I have previously written a book on the subject, titled *What in Hell Is Going On*. It questions what is going on in our society today, and what is happening worries me. Something is going on within our country that has been revolving in the past fifteen to twenty years but has dramatically quickened in the past few years. I was born in the roaring twenties, raised in the depression years of the thirties, only to reach maturity in the war years of the forties in time to participate in World War II, the greatest war of all times. It also was the war to end all wars. However, we've heard that before, shortly after World War I. In view of the state of the union these days, I can't help but to reflect on the past, and you know what, I believe I enjoyed life better then than I do today. I wonder what has happened to our traditional American values of God and country.

Statistics show most Americans are deeply conservative and Christian, yet it seems we have lost control—lost control to something called the progressive liberals who are determined on removing God from our daily lives in our own country. There are a number of reasons for the decline, but let me just state one man's opinion on who to blame and see if you don't agree. In our traditional past, we would go into the voting booths and cast our vote for our favorite candidate, Republican or Democrat. Many of us who are Republicans come from parents who, years ago, were Democrats and vice versa. But gone unnoticed was a movement in both parties commonly referred to as right and left. It's the progressive left that we should have been paying attention to. If we had, we would never have elected the likes of a Bill Clinton. We have had scandals in the past, but let's face it, there was never anything like the corrupt Clinton administration. After the Nixon-Ford administration, I can see why we went overboard and put in a Jimmy Carter. The country was ready for anything. But after four years of inept leadership, Jimmy couldn't be reelected even if he ran unopposed. So we made a change again. This time, I think we did pretty well with our choice of Ronald Reagan, and even the elder George Bush wasn't too bad. I felt confident that the country had righted itself. But Clinton was another matter. We already had an idea of his sordid background in his days in Arkansas. But we didn't seem to care. Looking back a few years, we survived some scandals of past administrations of Franklin D. Roosevelt, John F. Kennedy, Lyndon B. Johnson, Warren

Harding, and way back to Thomas Jefferson—maybe even Dwight D. Eisenhower. Maybe there are others. But how did we ever survive Bill Clinton? Reviewing his past, you'll find one arrogant character that defies all logic. He lied under oath about his sexual affair with Monica Lewinsky in the Oval Office. His cover-up attempt of the scandal was the beginning of the mounting evidence of deep corruption. It has to be considered among the most corrupt in the history of the republic. Yet we citizens remain apathetic as one of many TV commentators said, "Sure, something happened between Bill Clinton and Monica Lewinsky," but even if the president has done everything he's accused of, at worst, he's a hypocrite. So what, get over it? And this is when it all began. Get over it. If the president can do it, so can I. Who cares? It was at this time, when America adopted the so-what attitude, that we began a downward spiral, and look at what is happening in Washington today because we didn't care—the beginning of socialism and, close behind, communism. Mr. Obama (if still in office) might do well to take up skiing, then he too can go downhill with the rest of the country. Wake up, fellow citizens.

IS AMERICA GOING SOCIALIST?

GET YOUR HEAD OUT OF the sand, America! The world is going crazy, and the inmates are running the show! In doing some research on the subject, I came upon this little bit of wisdom. Norman Mattoon Thomas (November 20, 1884-December 19, 1968) was a leading American socialist, pacifist, and six-time presidential candidate for the Socialist Party of America. Socialist Party candidate for president of the United States Norman Thomas said this in a 1944 speech: "The American people will never knowingly adopt socialism but under the name of liberalism they will adopt every fragment of the socialist program, until one day America will be a socialist nation without knowing how it happened." He went on to say "I no longer need to run as a presidential candidate for the Socialist party. The Democratic party has adopted our program." In a

Frank A. Kaye

nation of over three hundred million citizens, I wonder how many of the current population would recall or have even heard of Mr. Thomas, much less care what he said. After all, this dates back to 1944. But then, not many of us heard of or paid attention to a narcissist named Barack Obama either. Just look at what has already transpired in just a few short months, and I'm talking present-day history. Nevertheless, although viewed by most Americans as a UN-savory form of politics, it is happening while we remain in a deep slumber. And this is only the beginning. We are seeing what appears to be a planned collapse of America, and the average American citizen remains too apathetic, too preoccupied with frivolity, and too self-absorbed to care enough to take action. I have recently reviewed a copy of the United States Constitution and read it completely. What a beautiful piece of literature it is. It clearly does not permit the government to do something it should not do. As a free people, we have never been closer to becoming subject to a one-man rule as we are today. So where do we go from here? I'm beginning to lose understanding and confidence in the strategic purpose of the current administration and am in constant search for answers; thus, I have come to just one conclusion. Despite the bleak outlook on our traditional way of life, we should not despair. We must all take a refresher course on the limits placed on what the government can and cannot do by the Constitution, then make use of the last remaining tool in the tool shed: the voting machine—where we, the people, can reverse this liberal movement and take back our country. You've heard it before, but it's worth repeating—take back our country.

WHY I CHOSE TO BECOME AN INDEPENDENT

SIMPLY BECAUSE I NO LONGER believe in the two-party system and believe independent thinkers who are losing faith in the American system will eventually become the largest voting bloc in the nation. That's why.

If you take the time to analyze the rhetoric by a potential candidate, it is a broken record. Promises, promises, promises. Promises they will not keep because the system will not allow it. American people are not stupid; we are determined, aggressive, intelligent, and loyal to the cause. We demonstrated that when we rallied around the flag in 1941. From a sleepy Sunday afternoon, we suddenly entered a global conflict, and four years later, we came home and showed the world our mettle;. However, unless we are faced with a major catastrophe, we are slow to act. We have now recognized the deficit in ethics and decency among our elected legislators and are ready to react. It seems we have, in recent years, become somewhat complacent and apathetic as we have been blindsided to how Washington works. Now time is running out. Our patience is exhausted; our intelligence has been insulted, and we have been taken for granted. Enough is enough. Traditional democracy as we know it is in danger of falling apart. It is time for Americans to wake up and once again rally around the flag.

Out of a nation of over 300 million people, only 100 senators, 435 congressman, 1 president, and 9 Supreme Court justices in all the so-called fellow Americans who we, the citizens, vote for and send to Washington to directly, legally, and morally guide our country to greatness, have, since World War I, screwed up this country almost beyond recognition. How did we allow this to happen? When running for political office, these future leaders come from all walks of life.

They are doctors, lawyers, dentists, and business executives. They are bright, intelligent, articulate, honest, well-spoken, and surefire representatives and are very convincing. But when sent to Washington, they quickly forget why they were sent there in the first place. Wasting no time, they quickly become part of the gang. See no evil, hear no evil, and say no evil of those they see committing evil. They reach for the back scratchers and cozy up to the lobbyists, the big-money donors, and the sweetheart deal makers and soon become self-serving politicians, despicable at best. And while counting their blessings, they become completely numb to the voices of their constituents. Members of both parties alike. Not to mention their disregard of personal and ethical behavior as demonstrated by scandals of all varieties from all corners of the country. We have tax cheats, sex offenders, politicians sitting in jails, and those that feed us a lot of lip gloss, deception, and exaggeration. The traditional American system needs a change. And it won't happen by way of the voting machine.

It seems inconceivable to me that a nation of over three hundred million citizens can allow this handful of leaders to foul up this country this bad and continue to reap all the benefits and perks they can lay their hands on while also allowing them to go on their merry way with pensions for life. Voting them in or out of office does not seem to solve the problem.

We've done this before. Substituting the players doesn't change the team. The system is broke, and it's time for a change.

Am I an angry white man? You betcha! I didn't pick up the gun in defense of my country in 1943, leaving behind my widowed mother with no visible means of support, to return home and see my country go down the drain. I served proudly in combat along with fifteen million other young men and women, then returned to a proud and victorious nation that now seems to have deteriorated and is scorned by many of the same nations that we went to war for. I am not a racist. I have no platform from which to dictate policy or make political decisions. But I do have opinions. And it is my opinion that aliens who broke the law to enter the USA have no right to claim any social benefits that belong to Americans. I believe America, as we know it, is in deep trouble with its generous giveaway programs for illegal aliens and foreign countries while American citizens, and particularly veterans, are bogged down in bureaucratic red tape and falling through the cracks. Perhaps this is why I feel resentful and outraged when I must get in line and fight for my veteran's rights while my country spends $338 billion a year on illegal aliens that have created such an adverse impact on our society. In the past eight years, this nation provided more than $16 billion in food assistance for tens of millions of people around the world, dedicated nearly $1 billion to improve sanitation and water supplies to developing nations, and committed $5.5 billion to address hunger and to help with global food crises. I am distressed at the $10 billion aid for Afghanistan, $40 million food aid for North Korea, $700 million aid package for Africa, billions to Columbia, and the beat goes on. While here in America, we support one another by charitable contributions and continue to struggle with homelessness, food stamps, welfare, health care, foreclosures, and veterans having difficulty obtaining disability compensation. Now add the ridiculous bailout program that we are currently engaged in. An Associated Press story tells us of some 691,000 children going hungry in America and close to one in eight Americans struggling to feed themselves adequately even before this year's sharp economic downturn. Overall, thirty-seven million Americans are living in poverty as reported by the agricultural department. Can you imagine some American being homeless after reading of the billions we spend on foreign soil? Does this not raise the hair on the back of your neck? Nor am I too pleased when I dial a number and must press one for English. Have we all gone off our rocker in this country? And what else has the elite 545 jet-setters got us into? They failed to stem the tide of illegal immigration, don't know how to seal our borders, but turn a deaf ear to the patriots who live there and are telling them how to do it. Same-sex marriages, courtrooms ruling that homosexuals have the constitutional right to practice sodomy, and rules that are destroying the fabric of our society and tearing our nation apart are among their proud achievements. These also include restricting school prayers, condoms issued to high school students, flag burnings, abortions on demand, and right to Pledge of Allegiance. How did they allow these radical forces to corrupt America's public education system from the elementary to the college level this way? Our children are being brainwashed in school or even in the privacy of their own bedrooms, watching TV bombarded with programs that promote crime, violence, and sex. How did they allow the runaway liberal judges to rule that reciting the Pledge of Allegiance in public schools was an unconstitutional endorsement of religion because it contains the words "under God"?

Is there moral decay in America? I'd say so. Hardly an adequate word can be added to the subject of decaying decency and moral values in America to those written by former US senator Zell Miller in his book *A Deficit of Decency* and to those written by political pundit Dick Morris in his book *Outrage*. Their revelations on the abuses perpetrated on the system by our duly elected representatives are beyond the absurd. Is there any doubt there is an anti-American undertow taking place in the country and, in fact, has established its dominance across the country? Does this not, in fact, coincide with the teaching of Marxist theoreticians? And was it not the Soviet leader Nikita Khrushchev, when visiting the United States in the sixties, who defiantly stated, "We will crush you from within," taking control of our infrastructure without firing a shot and utilizing our own tools in the process? Infiltrating our school system and electing liberal judges are but a small part of their success of influencing our system. But infiltrating the entertainment industry, particularly the TV and print media, is their most powerful accomplishment of what I believe is a planned collapse of our form of democracy. Is this the end? I pray not. But something has to be done. Someone must step in. It's up to you, America. We no longer can be apathetic, preoccupied, and self-absorbing. We are at war. In the meantime, I will remain optimistic, committed to the belief that things will get better in this—the greatest country on the globe. Because we, the American people, will make it happen. God, bless America—please.

AMERICA, THE POWERHOUSE

There is no argument that America has the most powerful military in the world. We have the largest defense budget in the world, allowing us to maintain a first-class army, navy, air force, marine corps, and coast guard. Comprised of approximately 1,500,000 highly trained volunteers with another 1,000,000 in reserve, these forces are equipped with the most sophisticated killing weapons ever designed by man. So great an inventory of weapons, that to list them could be a book in itself.

Our military services are led by the commander in chief who designates a secretary of defense who then consults with a national-security panel consisting of the seven-member joint chiefs of staff. I'm not sure I favor this powerful military to be under civilian control. Nevertheless, how would you rate this type of power against the current adversary who many of us don't even know what to call them?

WHY ARE WE FIGHTING A TWELVE-YEAR WAR?

AFTER WATCHING THE DESTRUCTION OF the twin towers live on national TV on September 11, 2001, with millions of other viewers, who would dare to question the reason for this war? However, it's the length of the time taking to win it that disturbs me. A stunned America was quick to learn that we were attacked by nineteen terrorists called the Al Qaeda, a fanatical group shielded by a tribe called the Taliban in a country called Afghanistan, led by an Osama bin Laden (now a dead man). A leader frequently seen on TV coming down from a rugged mountainside, garbed in rags and with the assistance of a tree branch for a cane, Osama had previously threatened the United States and was well known to our military intelligence, but no one suspected this type of an attack. Retaliation was justified and had to be swift. (It wasn't swift, but we got him.) But what are we doing there twelve years later? I understand the nature of this war and the sacrifices made by so many and particularly those selected for multiple deployment, but I can't bear to see thousands of our men and women returning home with physical and mental wounds that will never heal and will worsen in time while the dead return in bodily form to be received by families who are reassured by selected officials that they have sacrificed for a worthy cause. It is time that this war came to an end.

Let us turn back the clock some seventy-two years to December 7, 1941, and review the mood of America at that time. It was a quiet Sunday afternoon. There was some war talk going around, but it was not the most important issue that day. For it was the day of a championship-football game between the New York Giants and my super favorite, the Brooklyn Dodgers. Yes, I said Brooklyn Dodgers. We did have a football team in those days. With my ears glued to the old cathedral-style Philco table-model radio and the Dodgers leading 7-0, nothing else in the whole wide world mattered. Not until suddenly, at 2:26 PM eastern standard time, the play-by-play of the game was suspended with a dramatic announcement. "Ladies and gentlemen, we interrupt this broadcast to bring you an important bulletin from United Press." Flash Washington. "The White House announces a Japanese attack on Pearl Harbor. Stay tuned for further developments as they are received." Any similarity here to 9/11? Further announcements came rapidly only to reveal the extent of the horrific damages and loss of life. America came alive; even one of the attacking Japanese admirals was quoted saying, "We have awakened a sleeping bear."

Unprepared as we were, never in American history have Americans rallied around the flag as we had after that attack. To make matters worse, two days later, Germany and Italy declared war on the United States. Both believed that we would be unable to wage war on two fronts.

On April 18, 1942, just four months after this disastrous and sneaky attack, the air force, led by Lt. Col. (and later general) Jimmy Doolittle, and a small flight of sixteen B-25 Mitchell bombers took off from the top of an aircraft carrier, the USS *Hornet*, and made a surprise of our own by conducting a raid over Tokyo. This raid was viewed by many as a major morale victory for the United States. It showed the Japanese that their homeland was vulnerable to air attack. In another three months, we were able to rebuild our devastated fleet sufficiently enough to meet and decisively defeat the same Japanese sea armada at Midway, a strategic US island under attack by the Japanese. This rapid retaliation permanently damaged the Japanese striking power. And Japan was forced to fight the rest of the war in her defense only.

Add to this unbelievable feat, we mustered all our resources to fight a four-year global conflict, defeating such formidable enemies as Germany and Italy. Both were sophisticated nations well equipped to wage war. The point I'm making here is that even while being completely unprepared for any war, we demonstrated to the rest of the world America's ingenuity and will when provoked.

Now it is the year 2012. America has become a very sophisticated and powerful nation—thanks to some of the decision making of former president Ronald Reagan who believed in a strong America. After the Korea and Vietnam experience, we have somewhat remained ready for any contingencies and thus have become a superpower. Our arsenal of killing machines boggles the mind. Being an air force buff, let me just cite one example: We maintain the most elite air force on the globe. Weapons like the air force Reaper, a drone aircraft the size of a jet fighter powered by a turboprop engine and able to fly at three hundred miles per hour and reach fifty thousand feet. It is outfitted with infrared, laser, and radar targeting and carries a ton and a half of guided bombs and missiles. And guess what? It requires no one on board. Its pilot will bomb targets from a video console stationed in a remote base some seven thousand miles away.

Now for a brief comparison to our enemy as told to me by a seasoned marine from a place called Hindu Kush Mountains along the Dar yoi Pomir River. It's not even a country. There are no roads. There's no infrastructure; there's no government. There are no factories, shopping malls, gas stations, fast-food restaurants, jobs—no nothing; it's a hellhole. And these are their fighting men: They call them Tajiks, Uzbeks, Turkmen, and even some Pushtuns. They are really living Huns. They live to fight. It's what they do. They have no respect for anything—not for their families nor for each other nor for themselves. The only resemblance to humanity is that they eat food and drink water. The Taliban are cunning—like jackals and hyenas and wolverines. They are sneaky and ruthless, but when confronted, they are cowardly.

OK! So maybe this is a harsh assessment. After all, someone among this tribe did devise the cunning attack on the twin towers, killing 2,976 of civilian population and causing an economic impact costing billions of dollars. The nutshell is that we are fighting an enemy that does not have an air force, navy, army, or it would appear even have the intelligence or logistics to support one. We acted swiftly and should have devastated them immediately. Instead, we are in the twelfth year, dillydallying. I fail to understand the current strategy and planned-future strategy while we ask for bloodshed and sacrifice from our young men and women in the godforsaken land of Afghanistan. We sent to battle America's most dedicated, well-trained, experienced, and disciplined armed forces. Their proficiency and performance is unmatched and unquestioned. However, the leadership—uniformed, civilian, and elected—is questioned as the war goes on and the diplomatic malpractice continues.

Could this be a money war? Has anyone paid much attention to firms known as Halliburton or GE or even Boeing? Let's take it one at a time. Former president of the United States and five-star general Dwight D. Eisenhower, a product of the US Military Academy with a distinguished military career, gave his farewell message to the American people in which he stated, "In the council of government, we must guard against the acquisition of unwarranted influence, whether sought or unsought, by military-industrial complex. The potential for the disastrous rise of misplaced power exists and will persist." He was referring to the cozy relationship between some military suppliers and the government that awards their contracts. The military-industrial complex, as far as I am concerned, has to be watched as long as big money can be made in supplying defense needs.

I am saddened to see our young servicemen returning in flag-draped cases—as we call them nowadays. Solemnly being removed from one of our C-130s, this time there are only two, while in the back of my mind, I'm recalling the figure two—the latest two-billion-dollar contract awarded to the Halliburton firm for logistic support for this so-called war. Halliburton, founded in 1919, became the world's largest supplier of products and services to the oil and gas industry. This company controls over three hundred subsidiaries and employs over fifty thousand people based all over the globe. Their latest headquarter operation will be in Dubai in the United Arab Emirates. They maintain a telephone directory full of friends in high places, mostly in Washington. Is it a coincidence that this firm receives billions upon billions of dollars in sweetheart contracts? The severance package received by Dick Cheney, one of its executives, upon his resignation to run for vice president was in excess of thirty million dollars. I wonder what the others got. The company has a troubled history. It is laced with fraud, deception, and payoffs. Their performance and shady operations have been scrutinized by the usual politicians not in power. Then they too somehow join the team. It would seem Halliburton set aside their interest in oil and gas, seeing war profiteering as a more lucrative business by becoming the world's greatest logistic firm serving countries at war, currently supplying the war in Afghanistan with everything from Papa John's Pizza to basketball courts, including entertainment. See my point? Short wars don't pay. Even the most evil one of all, Osama bin Laden (now a dead man), purportedly remarked in one of his taped messages, "We must take in consideration that this war brings billions of dollars in profits to the major companies such as the Halliburton company. Based on this, it is very clear who is the one benefiting from igniting this war. It is the warlords, the bloodsuckers steering the world from behind a curtain." So said Osama bin Laden. What say you?

Now hear this from our own leader. The following is a narrative taken from a 2008 Sunday morning televised *Meet the Press*. The then-senator Obama was asked about his stance on the American flag. During the rendition of the national anthem, when the flag is displayed, all present except those in uniform are expected to stand at attention and face the flag with the right hand over the heart. Or at the very least stand and face it. Senator Obama replied, "As I've said about the flag pin, I don't want it to be perceived as taking sides. There are a lot of people in the world to whom the American flag is a symbol of oppression, the anthem itself conveys a warlike message. You know, the bombs bursting in air, and all that sort of thing." Obama continued. "The national anthem should be swapped for something less parochial and less bellicose. I like the song, 'I'd like to teach the world to sing' if that were our anthem, then I might salute it. In my opinion we should consider reinventing our national anthem as well as redesigning our flag to better offer our enemies hope and love. It's my intention, if elected, to disarm America to the level of acceptance to our Middle East brethren. If we, as a nation of warring people, conduct ourselves like the nations of Islam where peace prevails—perhaps a state or period of mutual accord could exist between our governments. When I become president, I will seek a pact of agreement to end hostilities between those who have been at war or in a state of enmity and a freedom from disquieting oppressive thoughts. We, as a nation, have placed upon the nations of Islam, an unfair injustice, which is why my wife disrespects the flag, and she and I have attended several flag burning ceremonies in the past.

"Of course now, I have found myself about to become the president of the United States and I have put my hatred aside. I will use my power to bring change to this nation, and offer the people a new path." This is from the president of the United States.

Now these words straight from his books! From the *Dreams from My Father*: "I ceased to advertise my mother's race at the age of 12 or 13, when I began to suspect that by doing so I was ingratiating myself to whites ... I found a solace in nursing a pervasive sense of grievance and animosity against my mother's race ... there was something about her that made me wary, a little too sure of herself, maybe and white ... it remained necessary to prove which side you were on, to show your loyalty to the black masses, to strike out and name names ... I never emulate white man and Brown men whose fates didn't speak to my own. It was into my father's image, the black man, son of Africa, that I'd packed all the attributes I sought in myself: the attributes of Martin and Malcolm, DuBois and Mandela."

Frank A. Kaye

And from his book *Audacity of Hope*, the most scary—"I will stand with the Muslims should the political winds shift in an ugly direction."

And we made him our president!

COMMANDER IN CHIEF, WHY?

I FIND IT IRRITATING TO the extreme when I see what looks like a picture-perfect marine, a young man obviously highly trained in the game of warfare and protocol and garbed in handsome dress blues, serving in the prestigious position of honor guard. His duties, among others, are to attend the arrival and departure of the president of the United States. He stands erect and renders a disciplined military salute. While the president, who also bears the title of the commander in chief of our armed forces, exits Air Force One or one of his helicopters in a blazer, wrinkled jeans, and an open-collar shirt and returns a lazy, sloppy, "Hi, buddy!"-type salute. It irks me even more when the commander in chief is a Barack Obama or a Bill Clinton—neither of whom have any understanding of military life since neither have served even one day in any branch of service and, in the case of Clinton, even evaded it. Article 2, section 1 of that sacred document called our Constitution states, "The executive power shall be vested in a president of the United States of America." It goes on and on and then says, "No one person except a natural born citizen, or a citizen of the United States, at the time of the adoption of this Constitution, shall be eligible to the office of President. Neither shall any person be eligible to that office who shall have not attained the age of 35 years and have been 14 years a resident within the United States." That's all there is, folks. Nothing more. So where are the qualifications for commander in chief of all the armed forces?

- Section 2 goes on to tell us that the president shall be commander in chief of the army and navy of the United States and of the militia of several states when called into service of the United States. However, the Constitution of the United States may give you the title, but it doesn't guarantee the brain or courage to command them. Since the Constitution was drawn up in the era of our great first president, George Washington, who had an established and great military mind from participating in a number of historic battles, I believe that the framers of this great document had in mind that all future presidents would be from military backgrounds. Not so. The next president, John Adams, turned out to be somewhat of a scholar far removed from any military experience, yet no one saw fit to immediately rule out the automatic commander-in-chief title that came with the duties of the president. Since then, we have had forty-four presidents in the executive office of which only twenty-three had some military experience with ranks ranging from lieutenant to general, but only one who could be considered as a true commander in chief from his achievements in the military—the first to gain the rank of a five-star general and who led the entire military in World War II, General Dwight D. Eisenhower. Now figure this as it relates to the current commander, the previous one, and even one beyond that. It's the United States of America versus the Taliban. You will not need to research Jane's world-renowned authority on military weaponry to find that America is a superpower. We possess in our air force stealth aircrafts, drones, killer helicopters, fighters, bombers, and smart bombs capable of taking out a foe in his bedroom. We have nuclear aircraft carriers, nuclear subs with atomic missiles, and nuclear-powered destroyers in our navy. We have elite rangers and paratroopers in our army and the finest fighting men in our proud marines. And don't forget the navy seals. Plus other weapons that boggle the mind. All led by generals and admirals from a comfort zone in one of the largest buildings in the world, the Pentagon, with you-know-who in command. So why are we engaged in combat for what is now beyond twelve years with an enemy that does not have an air force, navy, marine corps, military bases, or factories? They dress in rags, ride on camels (if they have any), wear split-toe sandals, and plan their strategies from inside canvas tents. Since items in the Constitution have in the past been amended or superseded, it is not set in stone. Why not an amendment to remove that obligation and bestow on someone with better qualifications? I just can't handle an Obama, a Bill Clinton, or even the younger George Bush as commander in chief. Alternatively, maybe even a Nancy Pelosi, who at one time was in the possible position to become a president.

ANOTHER VOICE FROM THE INTERNET

FROM UNKNOWN? I AM REALLY concerned about North Korea's appointment of the "dear leader" Kim Jung, the youngest son to be the new leader of North Korea, a nuclear power. After all, Kim Jung Un had no military experience whatsoever before Daddy made him a four-star general in the military. This is a snot-nosed twerp who has never accomplished anything in his life that would even come close to military leadership. He hasn't even so much as led a Cub Scout troop, let alone coached a sports team or commanded a military platoon. So setting that aside, next they make him the "beloved leader" of the country. But then, who are we to criticize? Didn't we do the same? We took a community organizer who has never worn a uniform and made him our commander in chief. A guy who has never led anything more than an Acorn demonstration is now the leader of our country. Can you picture these two sitting at a negotiating table?

COMPILATION

I WROTE IN THE INTRODUCTION of this book that the opinions stated are my own as I understand the workings of the government and from the viewpoint of an everyday citizen.

The following is a compilation of Internet correspondence sent by people from all walks of life, commonly called citizens, and are not the works of this author. It is from these Americans where all the wisdom comes from—the court of public opinion.

There are many brilliant people out there someplace but certainly not in Washington. In compliance with their request to pass their messages on, I selected what I considered some of the wisest comments and opinions, and see if you don't agree that the people not in politics know best. The first is the wisdom from a gentleman we all know. He was once considered a presidential candidate.

I read the Lee Iacocca book *Where Have All the Leaders Gone?* and found I am not alone in my opinion of the inequities in our government. "Where is the outrage?" he asks. Then continues to point out all the stupidities that are taking place in government with no decent leadership in sight: deficit spending; a bloody war with no plan for winning, no plans for leaving; skyrocketing gas prices; our schools in a complete disaster; and failure on all borders in controlling illegal immigrants. These are among our biggest problems. Nevertheless, he concludes that America will remain strong and will survive.

From the contribution of Mr. Bill Cosby, who offers his platform as a write-in candidate for the presidency. He would ban the phrase "press one for English" in our current-day telephone conversations. The Pledge of Allegiance will be said every day at school, and the national anthem would be played at all appropriate ceremonies. He would restore Social Security to its original state. "If you didn't put nuttin in it you ain't getting nuttin out." Welfare checks will be handed out on Fridays only and only after a successful completion of a urinalysis test for drugs. Mr. Cosby offers his apologies if he stepped on anyone's toes; nevertheless, he concludes with a "God bless America."

Alan Simpson, senator from Wyoming and cochair of Obama's deficit commission, calls senior citizens the greediest generation as he compared Social Security to a milk cow with 310 million teats.

And here is a response in a letter from Patty Myers in Montana. She also tells it like it is. "I have been paying S.S. taxes for 48 years, since I was 15. I am now 63. For starters I ask? As a career politician, you have been on the public teat for 50 years. How much money have you earned from the American taxpayers during your pathetic 50 year political career? At what age did you retire from your pathetic political career, and how much are you receiving in annual retirement benefits from the American taxpayers? And how much do you pay for your government provided health insurance?" I think she has the right to ask, don't you?

From the wisdom of Mr. Ben Stein comes the following: "Fathom the hypocrisy of a government that requires every citizen to prove they are insured, but not everyone must prove they are a citizen." Now add this: "Many of those who refuse, or are unable, to prove they are citizens will receive free insurance paid for by those who are forced to buy insurance because they are citizens."

From the article "Is Anyone in Washington Minding the Store?" by Nancy Cordes (CBS NEWS). "As gas prices spike and confidence in the economy plummets, Americans looking to Washington for help would find no one is minding the store," reports CBS news congressional correspondent Nancy Cordes. Ten senators left for China along with their spouses and military escorts. Their taxpayer-funded, ten-day trip includes meetings with Chinese leaders and a quick side trip to gambling mecca Macao, home to several casinos operated by companies in Democratic leader Harry Reid's home state of Nevada.

Four more senators, including Republican leader Mitch McConnell, are traveling through South Korea, India, and Afghanistan.

A glimpse at the congressional calendar shows why it has been so hard for members to get things done. Of the seventy-eight weekdays since January, the house has been in session only forty-four days—the senate only forty days. There's been an attendance rating just over 50 percent.

The president has also been out of town, raising millions for reelection in California. Members of Congress insist they need to take all these days off so they can spend more time in their home districts. It's going to be tough for them to come up with a compromise on the deficit if they are so rarely there to negotiate.

These are the highlights from a letter written by a fourth-grade teacher giving her viewpoint to our president.

> I have had it with you and your administration, sir. Your conduct on your recent trip overseas

has convinced me that you are not an adequate represented of the United States of America. You are not responsible to the peoples of any other country on earth. I personally resent that you go around the world apologizing for the United States. You evidently do not understand or know the history of the 20th century? Where do you get off telling a Muslim country that the United States does not consider itself a Christian country? Your bowing to the King of Saudi Arabia is an affront to all Americans. You can't find the time to visit the graves of our greatest generation because you don't want to offend the Germans but make time to visit a mosque in Turkey. I resent that you take me and my fellow citizens as brain-dead and not caring about what you idiots do. We are all watching what you are doing and we are getting increasingly upset with all of you. I promise you that I will work tirelessly to see that you do not get a chance to spend two terms destroying my beautiful country sincerely Ms. Kathleen Lyday, Hillsboro, MO.

On Where Your Money Goes

It's easy to dismiss individual programs that benefit noncitizens until they are put together and this picture emerges. Someone did a lot of research to put together all this data. Often these programs are buried within all the programs, making them difficult to find. Did you know that eleven billion to twenty-two billion is spent on welfare to illegal aliens each year by state governments? Twenty-two billion dollars a year is spent on food-assistance programs such as food stamps, WIC, and free school lunches for illegal aliens. Also, $2.5 billion a year is spent on Medicaid for illegal aliens. Twelve billion dollars a year is spent on primary and secondary school education for children here illegally. Seventeen billion dollars a year is spent for education for the American-born children of illegal aliens known as anchor babies. Three million dollars a day is spent to incarcerate illegal aliens. Thirty percent of all federal-prison inmates are illegal aliens. Ninety billion dollars a year is spent on illegal aliens for welfare and social services by the American taxpayers. Two hundred billion dollars a year in suppressed American wages are caused by the illegal aliens. In 2006, illegal aliens sent home $45 billion in remittances to their country of origin. The dark side of illegal immigration is that nearly one million sex crimes are committed by illegal immigrants in the United States.

How do we allow those in the United States Congress to get away with doing this year after year? Someone please tell me what the hell's wrong with all the people that run this country! Both Democrats and Republicans, we're broke and can't help our own seniors, veterans, orphans, homeless, etc. In the last few months, we have provided aid to Haiti, Chile, Pakistan, Libya, Egypt, and Turkey—literally billions of dollars! We pour hundreds of billions in dollars and tons of food to foreign countries while here, at home, we have people who are homeless, and according to the agriculture department, children that go to bed hungry.

Where Else Does Your Money Go?

Who among us has never heard of a pork barrel? It is a program by the federal government to provide funds for any project that your representative can dream of. In recent years, there were requests for a teapot museum, a bridge to nowhere, and the controversial Big Dig in Boston among other pet projects to serve self-interest and not the community for which it was intended.

But the biggest folly of them all has to be the National Endowment for the Arts—an agency of our government created in 1965 to offer support and funding for artistic excellence. Since its existence, it has been receiving annual funding from the US Congress, your dollars, from $160 to $180 million. Their interpretation of arts include art projects, art education, dance, music from opera to jazz, literature, musical theater, and all that jazz. The agency has been heavily criticized on a number of occasions for making grants to some real oddball, so-called talent. The artwork from one such nut was an exhibit of a plastic crucifix submerged in a vial of an amber fluid described by the nut as his own urine and was labeled *Piss Christ*. This was not an isolated event. There were many other controversial exhibits.

In 1981, then-president Ronald Reagan attempted to abolish this agency without success after a three-year battle.

In 1989, there were further attempts to do away with this wasteful agency for what was called anti-Christian bigotry by such notable figures as Republican senator Jesse Helms and Al D'Amato, later joined by prominent conservatives such as Pat Robertson and Pat Buchanan. Bottom line, the agency is still functional. Therein lies an example of your most important vote. Voting them in and out of the office does not change the game. The job does not get finished. In 1994, House Speaker Newt Gingrich renewed the attack on the NEA, which resulted in some cutbacks, but his attempt to eliminate the agency also failed. It appears the solution lies with we, the people. A massive letter-writing to your congressman might help.

You have just read some of the wisdom that comes through the Internet. The smart people are on the streets while the dummies are running our lives in Washington.

I have come to the conclusion that all the faults afflicting our society are not necessarily the faults of either the Republicans or the Democrats but that it lies directly in the system—a system with too many loopholes that promote corruption and deceit.

As of the success of corporate giants like Walmart and others, maybe we should seek future leaders from the business community. After all, America is a business.

A CHAPTER FOR OUR VETERANS

We write letters to the editors
As often seen or heard by the news media.

WE INTERRUPT THIS NARRATIVE ON the screwed-up politics taking place in America for a special chapter concerning our veterans. It includes the many letters written to the editors of local newspapers concerning veteran matters.

IMPROVING QUALITY OF LIFE OF VETERANS

THE AMERICAN RECOVERY AND REINVESTMENT Act, signed into law in February, provides—among other things—funds to improve claims and benefits processing. More specifically, it provides 150 million dollars for an increase in number of VA claims-processing staff in order to address the large backlog in processing veterans' claims—the number one beef among veterans caught in the maze of bureaucratic red tape.

In addition, it provides fifty million dollars to improve the automation of the processing of veterans' benefits to get benefits out sooner and more accurately. So where does it all go?

Frank A. Kaye

Millions in Bonuses Paid to VA Employees

Is that where it went? From the wire reports, we learn. Thousands of technology-office employees at the Veterans Affairs Department received a total of $24 million in bonuses over a two-year period—some under questionable circumstances, the agency's inspector general said in scathing reports that also detail abuses ranging from nepotism to inappropriate relationships.

The inspector general accused one recently retired VA official of acting "as if she was given a blank checkbook" as awards and bonuses were distributed to employees of the Office of Information and Technology in 2007 and 2008. OK! So maybe the generous giveaway was done before the American Recovery and Reinvestment Act was put into place. But who's to say if the scammers are not at it again? After all, I don't see any improvement in the system on any level. The snail pace in the processing of claims and their total lack of compassion for veterans needs is still prevalent. I am certain the awards policy is still in effect too. And bonuses are still being paid. Bureaucrats live on the fat of the land while the rest of us stay skinny, laboring to pay their salaries. But it is simply unacceptable that veterans are waiting longer and longer for benefits desperately needed while VA staff members, underworked and overpaid, get performance bonuses.

In my personal case, the slow pace and maze of paperwork added one more member to the ranks of the homeless. Despite repeated pleas of my critical situation, it had no effect on the so-called compassionate processors. And I lost my home. Is there any other way to approach the problem? Sure there is! Try contacting the American Legion, Disabled American Veterans, or maybe Veterans of Foreign Wars. And if that doesn't work, write to your congressman or either one of your two senators. Better still, write them both. And what do you get? As the Ernie Ford ballad says, "Another day older and deeper in debt." Plus a maze of confusing correspondence. Now pray tell, how can I go to a town hall meeting and still remain civil?

VETERANS NEED SOME ANSWERS

According to the Associated Press story, Secretary of Defense Robert Gates with Veterans Affairs secretary Eric Shinseki attended a mental-health summit in Washington where Gates said that troops injured in combat continue to face too many bureaucratic hurdles. Paperwork alone for them could be "frustrating, adversarial, and unnecessary complex." Earlier this year, they pledged with President Barack Obama to create a system that would make it easier for veterans to get disability benefits. The VA is struggling with a backlogged disability-claims system with hundreds of thousands of claims that need to be processed. He noted that a Rand Corporation study last year estimated that there could be more than six hundred thousand service members with brain and mental-health issues alone from the returning veterans.

May I respectfully suggest to Secretary Gates and Eric Shinseki that they consult with the secretary of the Department of Transportation, Ray LaHood, under whose department was created the Car Allowance Rebate System (CARS), colloquially known as cash for clunkers.

(Please pause with me here while I take my blood pressure pill.)

This program was designed to stimulate the economy, put over forty thousand new cars on the road, and place a big smile on the faces of thousands of auto dealers. With another two hundred thousand sales yet to be completed, the processing of dealer claims for rebates began on July 24 and concluded on August 24. In just thirty days, this program processed over 690,000 transactions and paid out a whopping 2,877 billion in rebates. "This is one of those programs you can really see working," said Rep. Candice Miller (R-MI). According to the DOT, the initial one billion dollars appropriated for the program was exhausted by July 30, but quickly an additional two billion dollars was appropriated by the House of Representatives with the senate approval one week later. The program concluded with Secretary Ray LaHood's comment: "It had been a thrill to be part of the best economic news story in America."

OK! So how did we get so efficient with this program but cannot find a solution to the VA backlog despite the American Recovery and Reinvestment Act. Is this a complete misjudgment of priorities, or is it pure neglect?

VETERANS NEED BETTER REPS

By Frank A. Kaye

IT ALL BEGAN IN THE days of the Civil War when Abraham Lincoln, one of history's better-known presidents, noting the hardship and sacrifices by veterans of wars, was to have said, "To care for him who shall have borne the battle, and for his widow and his orphan."

In later years, we were to hear others, such as President Harry Truman during the Korean Conflict, who said, "The debt to the Heroic men and valiant women in the service of our country can never be repaid!"

A few years later, it was President Lyndon B. Johnson, during the Vietnam era, who stated, "Our government and our people have no greater obligation than to assure that those that have served their country and the cause of freedom will never be forgotten or neglected."

And the latest remarks from one distinguished leader: "That in the end of the day, I must be able to look them in the eye and tell them truthfully that this generous and wealthy country has done everything possible for them" (Defense Secretary Robert M. Gates).

No matter what political persuasion or belief, Americans all are passionate about the government's sacred responsibility to care for those who have borne its battles. Will someone please inform the Veterans Administration?

After a five-year battle and a myriad of correspondence with the Veterans Administration to obtain service-connected compensation with no conclusion in sight, I turned to the leaders of state—senators, congressmen, military-department heads, and military-service organizations, which included the American Legion, Disabled American Veterans, Veterans of Foreign War's, etc. These organizations have specific goals in helping to cut through the maze of red tape of VA benefits, health-care eligibility laws, and other services that are due to them.

With negative results, I have concluded that the Veterans Administration has in place a set of ironclad rules with zero tolerance. Protected by some governmental power, they leave absolutely no room for deviation or common sense or leeway for someone in management to make their own decisions. Typically stated by one of our representatives, "I do not have the power to overturn or modify the Department of Veterans Affairs." So if our elected legislators, whom we call lawmakers, do not have the power to make any changes to this invincible department, then pray tell, who and how were these regulations put into effect in the first place? Moreover, how do we reverse them?

Thousands upon thousands of veterans seeking help in navigating through layers of bureaucratic red tape turn to their service organization for help and, usually as a last resort, turn to their elected legislators only to find in the final analysis that all they receive from theses reps is, at best, highly polished lip gloss in the form of a secretarial service.

In other words, BS. No one to my knowledge can penetrate the untouchable Veterans Department armor. Nor do they even try.

After a series of disappointments in dealing with the administration, I now thoroughly concur with Senator Tom Colburn (R-OK) and the ABC news report of August 28, 2008, on the workers at the federal government labeled "Missing in Action." This report tells us of the 2.6 million civilian workers on the federal payroll and the growing number of these workers who are absent without leave.

Tracked across eighteen government agencies from 2001 to 2007, the report indicated a complete lack of accountability and lack of discipline and further points a finger at the Department of Veterans Affairs as being among the worst violators, yet this department continues to ask for more employees. Is it any wonder that most veterans believe that the Veterans Affairs employees are underworked, overpaid, and insulated from the consequences of incompetence?

It is this writer's opinion that the employees in the Department of Veterans Affairs compensation sector lack the mind-set and work ethic required for careful and compassionate consideration in dealing with the hardships some veterans go through.

It's a sad day in America when an agency specifically created to aid and assist the veterans of this country cannot achieve its goals with more efficiency while bailing out the rest of the globe and providing luxurious accommodations to enemy combatants and neglecting our own veterans.

LETTERS TO THE EDITOR

The VA's Problems Lie in Washington Bureaucracy

I commend the handful of veterans who protested at the Savannah primary care clinic over unjust treatment received from the Veterans Administration. However, the impact was ineffective and quickly forgotten. Veterans' problems are not at a local clinic, particularly not at the Savannah facility, which is rated among the finest in the VA system. Veterans' benefits are being affected by the VA regulations solidly protected by an invisible shield of armor that is literally impenetrable and stems from Washington, DC. This is where the problem exists and veterans' claims are being delayed and denied. A million-man march to Washington might prove to be more effective. A swarm of appeal letters to your legislators is closer to home, but also ineffective. After a five-year battle and a myriad of correspondence with our president, senators, congressmen, the secretary of Veterans Affairs, plus numerous military-service organizations, nothing came except highly polished lip gloss in the form of a secretarial service.

Typically stated by one of our Georgia legislators, "I do not have the power to overturn or modify the Department of Veterans Affairs," this agency is rated by an accredited news-source investigation as one of the worst-performing bureaus in the system, lacking accountability and discipline. And it's staffed with personnel lacking the mind-set and work ethics required for careful and compassionate consideration in dealing with the hardships that some veterans go through.

Frank A. Kaye

To the Defeated, the Spoils

Editor

With all the talk on the budget deficit, welfare reform, governmental spending, etc., I wonder how many Americans, particularly Desert Storm troops, know our government is resettling in the United States four thousand Iraqi soldiers who surrendered in the Persian Gulf War. Each will receive cash grants of $7,000. Under federal-refugee guidelines, former POWs and their families are entitled to medical and welfare payments, including aid to families with dependent children, cash assistance for employment, and language-training programs, health assessments, and other continuing health services. All paid by our tax dollars. How about them apples?

Frank A. Kaye

Frank A. Kaye

Prison or Boot Camp?
A Veteran Explains to the Bleeding hearts How Discipline Works

Editor

At age eighteen, I was confined and restricted to a camp in sweltering Biloxi, Mississippi. My living quarters consisted of a single bunk bed with another one attached to the top of it in a long wood-constructed building with no air-conditioning—not even a fan. There were at least one hundred other guys in the building who were awakened at 5:00 AM to a shrill whistle and loud shouting. Upon this rude wake-up call, we were rushed in underwear to another building, approximately fifty yards away, called the latrine. It was there that we showered, shaved, and used the commode—all in the open undivided space. By 6:00 AM, we were marched in precision order to still another building called the mess hall where, after a long wait in line, we were served a meal of powdered eggs, hard toasted bread, and coffee on an oval-shaped metal-stamped plate called a mess kit. After rushing through this breakfast, you again stood in line to dip this kit in a series of three galvanized garbage cans that contained hot, greasy water to clean the kit. Diarrhea was not uncommon. Matters got even worse as we progressed to another phase of this program where we were confined in a heavily wooded area, sleeping in a two-man triangular-shaped cloth shelter called a pup tent, together with thousands of one-inch long mosquitoes and some snakes. No, I was not an inmate in a penal colony. I was a private in the honorable service of the United States Army Air Corps. I would like to bring this to the attention of the bleeding hearts. We are so critical of Georgia's correction commissioner whose mission is to toughen up the state prison system. I am certain the majority of law-abiding citizens approve of his methods.

Frank A. Kaye

A Wake-up Call

Editor

I fully support a strong America. But if the top brass in my beloved air force are trying to convince Congress on the worthiness of the B2 Bomber based on its stealthiness, then it's time to wake up. The technology we have today can evidently be purchased by the Russians tomorrow and from the best marketplace in the world—Washington, DC.

Frank A. Kaye

(Below caption was placed in a newspaper article in the original)

Veterans Usually Get Good Care at Local Clinic

I share similar experiences as those of fellow veteran Cavanaugh Murphy ("Local VA clinic doesn't show him much concern," Letters, April 19) as he related the excellent health care rendered at the different VA facilities.

But there is a difference of opinion with his negative comment about the careless attitude he encountered at the clinic in Savannah. I suggest that it was a misunderstanding and an isolated one at that.

I am a member of the American Legion, Veterans of Foreign Affairs, Disabled American Veterans, the Eighth Air Force Historical Society, and have been a patient at the clinic since 1992. As such, I am in constant contact with fellow veterans and am aware of many of their problems.

True, there is an occasional bump on the road, but overall, the services rendered at the Savannah VA clinic are as good as, if not better than, those experienced in the private sector. For other occasional glitches in the system, we should look to Washington for solutions.

Frank A. Kaye

Nothing from Our Leaders

Editor

Daily headlines tell us of the battle to balance the federal budget and finally, the bottom line, raise the taxes with some insignificant cuts mostly in the welfare sector with hardly a word on cuts like political salaries or the infamous $325 toilet seats, the $300 hammer, or the $40 bolts that the defense contractors have been ripping off Uncle Sam for years.

Twenty-seven Klansmen marched from the Washington Monument to the Capitol. This forty-five-minute march drew an estimated 1,200 demonstrators and closed down the Capitol. It took two thousand police officers in riot gear as well as 800 US capital police and 325 US park police in helicopters, on motorcycles, and on horseback. All 4,750 district officers were mobilized for this march at a cost estimated at $800,000. This is just for twenty-seven Klansmen—while I have to pay extra for my beer and gas. I don't believe we, the citizens, are getting anything from our leaders, Republican or Democrat. I am ticked off.

Frank A. Kaye

Service Records Don't Tell the Complete Story

As a combat-tested veteran of World War II, I have the deepest respect for all Purple Heart recipients.

But when John Kerry and his band of brothers decided to showcase the senator's Vietnam service in his quest for the White House, he obviously was not aware of the can of worms he was about to open.

He received three Purple Hearts in a four-month period, none of which required hospitalization or disability compensation. But they did earn him a ticket home. This is a hard sell.

Now, in the attempt to quell the backlash, Kerry and his staff tell people to look at the records. This won't cut it. Service records are hearsay and often erroneous.

Case in point: My buddy, Mark Schaefer, a Savannah resident and fellow WWII veteran, was shot down behind enemy lines, was injured, and spent two years, two months, and two days as a prisoner of war. Because of screwed-up reports, he was awarded and received his Purple Heart fifty-nine years later at a special ceremony in our Mighty Eighth Air Force Museum.

This is just one of many similar cases.

I believe the Swift boat guys got this one right.

Frank A. Kaye

Food Aid Needed in the United States, as Well as in Poor Nations

A recent article, as it appeared in the news, by the Associated Press, titled "Bush: Aid to poor nations especially necessary now," reads, "Amid global economic turmoil, President Bush said that it's more important than ever for the United States to help the less fortunate."

In a speech highlighting his administration's aid work, Bush said the United States has provided more than $16 billion in food assistance for tens of millions of people around the world, dedicated nearly $1 billion to improve sanitation and water supplies in developing nations, and committed $5.5 billion to address hunger during the next two years to help with global crises.

A few days later, another article by the Associated Press reads, "More U.S. children going hungry."

Some 691,000 children went hungry in America sometime in 2007 while close to one in eight Americans struggled to feed themselves adequately even before this year's sharp economic downturn, the agriculture department reported.

Will someone enlighten me, please?

Frank Kaye

Deficit Spending with Food Aid for North Korea?

Editor

I find it difficult to comprehend the intricate workings of our government. Recent correspondence from our congressman, Jack Kingston, informs us that we are paying $40 billion in interest on the $5.1 trillion national debt.

The same letter also stated that the Medicare Trust Fund is running out of money at a dangerous pace, spending $25 million more than it takes in each day.

Additionally, we daily read or hear of our domestic problems in welfare, the homeless, food stamps, the unstable Social Security programs, cutbacks in the Veterans Affairs Department, etc. We are also told that the average tax burden is now 38 percent of household income to support these failing programs.

So how come the State Department announced that the United States will resume $6.1 million worth of food assistance to North Korea? Is this the same North Korea we waged war against?

What a kick in the head to the American citizenry.

Frank A. Kaye

Senators: Govern First, Travel Later

The country is in an economic mess never seen before, and the nation's debt is about to hit the ceiling. I ask why are the first and second ladies of the land flying around in an Air National Guard jet for TV interviews in New York?

And why are a group of senators like Harry Reid and including our own Johnny Isakson, together with their spouses, taking a taxpayer-funded trip to China with a side visit to mecca Macao where there are gambling casinos owned by the same guys who operate in Nevada, Reid's home?

What's wrong with the people who are supposed to run this country?

Frank A. Kaye
Guyton

Frank A. Kaye

Veterans Need More Than VA Bureaucratic Red Tape

Your editorial on veterans deserving more than red tape is a welcomed commentary—moreover, is also appreciated by all veterans. The veterans' problem of bureaucratic red tape and nonsensical double-talk that sometimes requires the intervention of the district congressman whose office and personnel know the game is, as you stated, not really the solution. It's more like relating with a ventriloquist.

The veteran knows what the problems are; it's the correction to the problems that we seek, not a routine inquiry to inform the veteran what he already knows.

It appears this "know the game" staff simply deal with pretyped, routine correspondence—a quick fix without serious analysis of the problem.

Add to this a case in point: a letter to a legislator appealing for help in a serious financial crisis created by a VA cutback in compensation brought back a tin-cup letter from said legislator asking funds for his upcoming reelection campaign.

The problems needing correction are for the VA to add a little heart in their analysis, establish a priority system, improve the timeliness and accuracy of the claim-adjunction system, and add a better effort to make veterans aware of the current issues in their rights and benefits—particularly better access to their personal accounts.

Frank Kaye

FRANK A. KAYE

Editor

I am appalled at the amount of crybabies, dissenters, and yellowbellies that emerges when our country has a crisis. They forget that the people in Washington, DC, who run this country were put there by their own vote. If you don't like it, you have the opportunity to voice your opinion again on election day.

In the meantime, regardless of how unpopular the decisions may be, higher taxes or wars, they must have our support—united support, Republican or Democrat alike.

As a combat-tested veteran, I feel our troops don't want to hear bellies aching; they want support and encouragement. So rally around the flag. Put your heat in it or get out.

Frank A. Kaye

Cost of Freedom Was Dear to Many Veterans

Freedom is not free; veterans paid for it. It's not just a lapel button; it's a story. Being active with a veteran's group, we just paid a visit to the nursing home section of the Atlanta Veterans Administration Hospital.

That visit with an aging group of World War II veterans was a reminder of how little is known of those men outside the hospital walls.

I suggest that all our elected officials be compelled to make such a visit once a year.

It might alter their policy-making decisions, particularly the ones regarding future hostilities.

Frank A. Kaye

Frank A. Kaye

What About War Records of GOP Candidates?

The new Democrats of today paint a vivid portrait of John Kerry's war record as if that is a prime requisite to be the next president of the United States (but no mention of the Jane Fonda thing).

How quickly they forget that

- in the 1992 campaign, they completely discounted the war record of George Bush, a distinguished World War II veteran.
- in the reelection campaign of 1996, they played down and almost completely discounted the exemplary WWII record of Republican nominee Bob Dole, who carries his battle scars with him to this day.

Those war homes were pitted against the Democratic choice—often described by the media as a pudgy-faced Arkansas redneck with a history of financial and sexual scandals. He was depicted as a pot-smoking womanizer, draft dodger, and anti-war demonstrator, but look who won the election.

I believe something has gone wrong in the United States.

Frank A. Kaye
Savannah

BASIC SOLUTION TO OUR BUDGET DEFICIT

STOP SPENDING MONEY YOU DON'T have. One should have money before you spend it. You can't borrow yourself out of debt. What's good for the household is good for the government.

How did these no-brainers get us into a sixteen-trillion deficit? I can't help but wonder—why, with the situation that we are in, are we fighting a twelve-year war with an enemy who operates out of tents and caves? Why do we take money from those who work and give it to those who don't want to work? Why can you view pornography on TV and the Internet but oppose a nativity scene in a public park during the Christmas holidays? We spend millions to rehabilitate criminals but do nothing for the victims. We provide funds for organizations that kill unborn children through their abortion practices but find it wrong to execute a serial killer. And that's just the beginning of some of the absurd doings in Washington. We are now reportedly spending 338 billion on social programs for illegal aliens—add to this the absurd pork barrel spending with money we are borrowing. You do the math, fellow citizens. It's your money they are tossing around. In the last months, we have provided aid to Haiti, Chile, Turkey, and even Pakistan. Is this why we are in a deficit? I am appalled at the folly going on in the nation's capital. It is hard to believe what's happening to our country. Never before have we seen such fiscal irresponsibility.

Now a suggestion for a quick fix: one would get the impression that there isn't money in this country. We are broke, dead in the water. Not so, fellow Americans, not so. We have big bucks lying around, and I know where they're at. For starters, they are in the banks of the top-richest people in the world, and they all have philanthropic foundations. Warren Buffett, Bill Gates, Paul Allen, and the Walton family are but a few. There are billions in corporate America like the oil industry's Chevron, Exxon, Hesse, et al.; retailer's Walmart, K-Mart, Target, etc.; banking's JP Morgan, Bank of America;

defense industry's General Electric (sitting on billions yet paying no taxes), Boeing, and General Dynamics; insurance industry's American General, State Farm, Allstate; and the pharmaceutical's Johnson and Johnson, Pfizer. And this is only the beginning. According to the Center for Responsive Politics in Washington, DC, the labor unions in America are sitting on tons of surplus cash—ready to support their favorite political candidates. Why not a stimulus program in reverse? Since they all have philanthropic programs in place, why not include Uncle Sam among the recipients? Sizable donations or at least interest-free loans would help reduce our deficit. Any amount given would make small dents in their treasuries that would almost immediately be replaced by their constant twenty-four-hour cash flows. Case in point: the millions upon millions paid out by BP for damages caused by their recent oil-rig disaster were, by their own statements, replenished at the gas pumps in a few days. Vast amounts of money were earned by these conglomerates in this great country with not enough returning. To not repeat old habits of free, irresponsible spending, I would suggest representation on the governing board of the treasury department by some of the same business brains that created the wealth for the above that know how to make the money while elected officials only know how to spend it. LOST WISDOM FROM 2064 YEARS AGO.

"The budget should be balanced, the Treasury should be refilled, public debt should be reduced, the arrogance of officialdom should be tempered and controlled and the assistance to foreign lands should be curtailed lest Rome become bankrupt.

People must again learn to work instead of living on public assistance." Cicero (55BC)

FROM THE SCHOOL OF COMMON SENS-OLOGY:

ANOTHER SOLUTION TO AMERICA'S DEFICIT. I have always maintained that the solutions to most of the problems that plague this nation lie with the common people, those not in politics—the ones I call the court of public opinion. Have you ever played the game of Monopoly? Sure you have! Most of us had at some time or the other. So we all know that to begin the game, we must first remove the play board from the box and read the rules and regulations. That's called the beginning. And America needs a new beginning. Set aside the game for the moment and let's look at some interesting statistics: the *Forbes 400 Magazine* lists the top-ten billionaires in the country as Bill Gates, 59 B; Warren Buffet, 39 B; Larry Ellison, 33 B; Charles Koch, 25 B; David Koch, 25 B; Christy Walton, 24 B; George Soros,

22 B; Shelton Adelson, 21 B; Jim Walton, 21 B; and Alice Walton, 21 B.

Another report from the *Wall Street Journal* reveals that America has 5.2 millionaire households and approximately three million millionaires. Now take into account the top-ten wealthiest corporations: Exxon Mobile, Walmart, Chevron, Conoco Phillips, General Motors, General Electric, Berkshire Hathaway, Fannie Mae, Ford Motors, and Hewlett-Packard. This, dear readers, is just the tip of the iceberg of the enormous wealth in America. There is a lot more. Billions upon billions of dollars are earned from the most beautiful country in the world by people like you and me. They are sitting on it and earning more every day.

These are the kingpins, the rainmakers, the kingmakers. They have the know-how and control the megabucks. These are the people whose money, influence, and support are responsible for the leadership holding office in Washington today. We only contribute to the system with our vote. Obviously, some poor choices were made. Why else are we in a sixteen-trillion-dollar deficit? It's a deficit in leadership that created the problem. The game is over. The smart people in the corporate world win. The USA loses. We now need a rebirth in America. It's back to the game board; only this time, the game is different. It's not Monopoly; it's called a level playing field.

From within the enormous wealth and brainpower of those mentioned, they would create a new bank, USA #1. Since we like to give names to places and things, we would soon call it you-sa one. Additional capital for this bank would come from citizens who believe in the country since it would be an investment in the USA. The sole purpose of this bank is to grant or at least give interest-free loans to individual states for only one purpose. And that is for the infrastructure of that state. Each state in the union would then build superhighways, bridges, and dams; control raging rivers that periodically run out of control; protect its borders where needed; provide the best available hospitals and schools, police and fire protection, and recreational facilities; and add numerous other projects to improve life for its citizens. Get out of the way, Big Brother; we can do it better. And create unlimited employment in the process.

Every able-bodied man and boy, even the handicapped, would find employment. And the federal government would reap a fanatical income from our very current tax program. There would be no need for new taxes, no need for increase in taxes—just more citizens paying taxes.

With this new flow of taxes, Uncle Sam would quickly reduce its deficit, maintain only the armed forces, keep the Social Security system in place since the citizens would continue to contribute to the program, and care for its veterans who served in its many wars. We could streamline America by eliminating useless agencies. First, the department of education, with a projected spending for 2012 of 39 billion; department of labor, projected spending of 127 billion for 2012; and the department of energy, projected spending of 39 billion. Who needs them? It would then funnel the surplus back to USA #1 (you-sa one) for redistribution to states still in need and a return to the investors. Needless to say, a governing board of watchdogs from the successful corporate world would have to be appointed to oversee the federal idiots who created the mess in the first place.

You will note there is no mention of welfare. There just would be none since everyone would be working except for some isolated cases among the handicapped. Likewise, there is no mention of corruption. There too would be none since the penalties would be severe (life in prison for starters). That ought to keep the crooks in line. Overall, this plan would downsize the big government by placing more responsibility with the states. And we could consider firing the 435 congressman and 100 senators and save a lot more money.

ONE MORE BRAINER

From the school of common sense-ology: Just one more idea. Tax the rich. Tax the rich is the cry from Washington these days. It may sound good to those of us who are poor. But whatever happened to all men are created equal, that they are endowed by their Creator with certain unalienable rights. That among these is Life, Liberty and the pursuit of Happiness. And doesn't making money make you happy? Do you not have the right to make money and be able to keep it. This is stated in the Declaration of Independence. Which also states, that whenever any form of government becomes destructive of these ends, it is the right of the people to alter or abolish it, and to institute new government. Take note Mr. President, you may be reaching out too far.

Moreover, these are the people mention previously as the king makers, the power house leaders, the brainers who know how to make the big bucks. You will not take any of it away without a fight. They will find the loop holes and means to supplement whatever you take away from them. Most likely they will recover it by price increase in the merchandise they produce and ultimately Joe Six-Pack and the soccer Mom will pay the price.

But, there is a better way and that is to tax the corporations that they have created under the liberal policies of the good old U.S. of A. And use these same corporations as a shield to protect the huge surplus of cash they are sitting on.

Case in point: General Electric Corporation

When in the history of America have you ever imagined of an executive on the managerial level get canned but receive a multi-million dollar severance package. Who ever imagined a baseball player, tossing a four inch ball around earning 20 million bucks? All paid for by we the people at the gates and check-out counter. How much more of this absurdity can the consumer take?

Imposing a larger tax on the corporations is the idea but does not completely solve the problem. Don't forget who run these corporations. It is the big buck guys mentioned above. They stand loaded with many tricks to combat any attempt by any regulation that may hurt their income. Among which is the powerful influence they possess by way of the lobbyist they pay for and control. Once again, they will find a way to trickle it down to the consumer. It is one vicious cycle that just goes spinning around but carefully controlled by those on the top.

Now comes the answer from street level politics. Take one at a time. My favorite rip off corporation. The oil industry. By their own statements, BP, we all know who BP is don't we? They stated, that the high fines imposed upon them for the disastrous oil spill in the Gulf is rapidly recovered by the constant cash flow at the pumps. So this is where we stop the spin of their wheel. Listen up Washington. Go full blast and impose your tax hike on corporate America. They simply have too much. But you must also put a freeze on their retail products. Only then can we continue to play the game on a level playing field.

If the thought of why we are in such a mess ever occurred to you, please read on.

LOOK WHO'S RUNNING THE SHOW

I THINK GOOD OLD HARRY Truman hit the nail right on the head when he observed, "My choice early in life was either to be a piano player in a whorehouse or a politician." And to tell the truth, there's hardly any difference. I, for one, believe the piano player job to be much more honorable than current politicians Marion Barry, Mark Sanford, Larry Craig, Elliott Spitzer, John Edwards, and John Ensign. The list goes on. All elected officials, Republicans and Democrats alike, black and white, east and west—it makes no difference where they come from. All have been involved in perverted sex, lies, deceptions, and scandals.

Is there any wonder why America has lost its prestige and respect throughout the globe? In view of the state of the union these days plus the continuous flow of illicit behavior by our elected officials, I would like to send to every elected politician on every level of government Washington's prayer for the nation (first written at Newburgh on June 8, 1783, and sent to all governors of all the states) if only I could afford the postage.

> Almighty God, we make our earnest prayer that thou wilt keep the United States in thy holy protection, that wilt incline the hearts of the citizens to cultivate a spirit of subordination and obedience to government, and entertain a brotherly affection and love for one another and for their fellow citizens of the United States at large. And finally that thou wilt most graciously be pleased to dispose us all to do justice, to love mercy and to demean ourselves with that clarity, in pacific temper of mind which were the characteristics of the Divine Author of our blessed religion and without a humble imitation of whose example in these things, we can never hope

to be a happy nation. Granted our supplication, we beseech thee, through Jesus Christ our Lord amen.

PS: And please, Lord, restore the moral values and decency of our leaders.

CONVENTION TIME

IT WAS JUST A COINCIDENCE that this manuscript was about to be put to bed when the Republican and Democratic conventions came upon us—a moment so eagerly awaited by all the political buffs. And so we took a break, sat back to watch all the actors perform, and a performance we did see. What a field day for the comic writers. I have never heard so much bovine excrement piled up in one place at any given time by both parties. Although through it all, it seems that the Red and Blue did agree on one common issue. They all repeatedly reminded us that we live in the greatest country in the world. I'll buy that anytime. But then came the rest of the story as they related one by one their plans on how to further screw it up.

Frank A. Kaye

From the Red Side of the Story

Promises, promises, promises—what else is new? Take a look at the breakdown. Since the days of Calvin Coolidge, our thirtieth president (1923), we have had forty-four years of Democratic and forty-five years of Republican—nearly evenly divided leadership in the White House. We change parties and substitute players but play the same game. There is nothing new here. Inaccurate and misleading statements from both sides are each geared to make the other look bad. The difference noted was that the Republicans now seem a little bit more conservative and the Demos moved far to the left.

Heard Clint Eastwood, Hollywood superstar say that "not everyone in Hollywood is to the left." That was hard to swallow. The rest of his shtick was pretty entertaining.

From the Blue Side

Seeking some applause, I heard one guy say to those still awake, "You are the greatest generation in the world" (mild applause). How quickly he forgot Tom Brokaw's greatest generation of the twenties. Another one was a promise of mandatory sixty-mile-per-gallon vehicles down the road but offered no guarantees that gas prices would not be ten dollars per gallon. I heard some fancy figures tossed about too—trillions, billions, millions—as if anyone still awake had any idea what a trillion looks like. No human being in the world ever accumulated a trillion dollars in his lifetime. We also heard from a former Florida governor who was once a Democrat but switched to be a Republican and now is an independent who supported the Republican candidate but now supports B. O. What in the world was that all about? I couldn't pass on the ranting and raving of the blonde, former Michigan governor and her theatrics. For a while, I thought I was seeing Howard Dean in drag, repeating his Iowa act. Remember him?

Oh yes, I knew he'd be there—the self-proclaimed war hero from the Vietnam era, sporting his four-hundred-dollar haircut. He made some comments that quickly bombed out since they had no substance.

I had to agree with some of the comments by the senate candidate from Massachusetts, the so-called warm-up act for Bill Clinton. She said the system is rigged, pointing her finger on the billions in profit made by the oil companies, while we get snookered at the pumps. The rest of her stuff was simply BS.

I took some interest in the message by the greatest con man in the world who, in the process of promoting B. O., paved the way for his wife's bid for the big job, which comes with another four years. I don't believe he ruled himself out for some future big deal either. However, I must admit his presentation was very effective and well rehearsed. But then again, that's what a con man does.

And from Mr. Big himself, a promise of one million new jobs in the next four years—that's good. What happens to the twenty-two million still unemployed? On the success of the GM stimulus, that's good! Where is the payback? I heard a lot of bull on outsourcing too. Let's see if I got that one straight. A view from the street: after some extensive travel throughout the southeast region of the country, we noted a great deal of garment-making factories producing mostly men's shirts and underwear. These jobs were sewing buttons, collars, and labels on men's shirts bearing American-name brands. Minimal in pay but it kept many locals employed and helped a small community thrive. Then came the powerful unions with big-buck demands, and offshore they went—Mexico, Guatemala, Belize, and even China—where labor is much cheaper. Is this what you call outsourcing? In the meantime, also noticed were BMW autos being built in Spartanburg, South Carolina; Japanese Honda cars being built in Tennessee; Korean Kia autos built in Alabama; Japanese Bridgestone tires with facilities in South Carolina and Georgia; French Michelin tires and German Continental tires also in South Carolina; Sony Industries all over the country; and Mitsubishi in Georgia. Do you suppose the people in those countries are also talking of outsourcing? I'd say that is a pretty good trade-off. You make our underwear; we'll do the big-buck jobs.

Finally, the big event of the evening was the balloon drop where most of the hot air was stored during the three-day blowout. There were lots of noise, lots of hugging, lots of drinking, and lots of kissing. I saw one delegate kissing his own wife, and there was lots of packing for the trip back to the campaign trail for more bull, distortions, accusations, and name-callings.

ARE YOU MAD YET?

I BET YOU ARE. YES, you are. I know I am. Everyone is. At least all the folks I talk to are. With the direction in which our country is heading in these days, it seems everyone is mad. And this, my friends, is not good for you, not according to my psychiatrist. He suggests you cool it, which makes me grateful that we have in our system the freedom to express ourselves. We can vent our frustrations and get things off our chests in writing a book such as this and hope that it may make an impact on some of the readers. It may awaken some citizens to come up with better ideas like the recent birth of the Tea Party, which has brought to life some old-fashioned patriots. But if anything else, it's still better than beating your head against a brick wall, right?

To me, it is a form of therapeutic value. When I write, I feel relaxed. Try it sometime.

Something is going wrong in this country, and I wonder how it can be changed. Americans cannot remain silent while our country is being systematically destroyed as one party grows in unbridled power. Anger makes your mouth work faster than your mind, so maybe we should resort to an alternative measure. Besides, he who blows his stack adds to the world's pollution, and we have enough of that. Nevertheless, outrage must be heard, and something has to be done—something like the Tea Party movement or like what happened in a recent election in Massachusetts and repeated in Houston, Texas, where it would appear that the patriotic spirit is reborn. What is it that makes us so mad, I ask. For starters, what in hell does the government do to make us happy? We have 535 voting members in the legislative process that makes this country function, a system that has been in existence for a whole lot of years, and you know something? We, the people, put them there. It is our fault, and now it seems we cannot do anything about it, and that makes us mad. I looked to one of my US senators for some answers, and he tells me, "I, as a US senator, do not have the power to overturn or modify another agency's decision." My other senator—we have two, you know—although I wonder at times where these wise men are, makes a similar statement. Other politicos refer my correspondence to the same agencies that I complain about, and still others don't even bother to answer. Try writing to the president! If these elected officials cannot make decisions and effect changes, then why in the hell do we keep them there? Now look at their accomplishments: The US postal system, established in 1775, 235 years later, it is broke. Social Security, established in 1935, 74 years to get it right, and it is broke. Fannie Mae, established in 1938, 72 years to get it right, and it is broke. Medicare and Medicaid, established in 1965, 44 years to get it right, and it is broke. Freddie Mac, established in 1970, 39 years to get it right, and it is broke. The department of energy created in 1977 to lessen our dependency on foreign oil, 33 years to get it right, and we now import more oil than ever before. And then there is my favorite, the Veterans Administration.

In 1636, the pilgrims passed a law that stated that the disabled soldiers would be supported by the colony; this was a form of a veterans' administration in existence at that time. On March 15, 1989, the Department of Veterans

Administration was established as a cabinet-level position and hailed by then George W. Bush the elder as saying, "There is only one place for the veterans of America, in the Cabinet room, at the table with the president of the United States." Wow! Tell me that isn't an important bureau! If you do the math, that would be 376 years of America caring for its veterans. And yet this administration can't seem to do it right. An ABC report shows the inefficiencies in this department are rated at probably the lowest of all governmental agencies.

Now, how would you rate the operations of a corporation like Walmart to our government?

What else makes us mad? Well, there is the twelve-year war going on thirteen. I know why we are there, but I question the leadership conducting it. I don't even know what to call the enemy. Al Qaeda? Taliban? Terrorist? They have no country, no army, navy, air force—nothing. They live in caves, plan their attacks in tents, yet they raise holy hell throughout the globe. I do know that in 1941 we were at war with very capable and sophisticated enemies, Germany and Japan, and it took all our resources and four years to become victorious. But these cave dwellers confuse my logic.

Yesterday's headlines tell me American forces, with our many innovative ways to kill, dispatched a multimillion-dollar, pilotless drone over a selected target, unleashed a multimillion-dollar, sophisticated, radar-guided missile, and successfully killed one very important Taliban leader.

Today's headline tells me of a suicidal female Al Qaeda bomber laden with a makeshift bomb belt who walked into a building, set herself off, destroyed the entire building, and killed approximately forty people. Total cost was about ten bucks.

I'm also hearing of American destroyers patrolling Florida waters to fend off attacks by pirates. Pirates? Did I read this right? Pirates in rowboats? Is this for real? Or am I reliving Errol Flynn in the *Captain Blood* movie?

Now I'm looking at some reports on pork barrel spending, and the hair on the back of my neck begins to bristle. But then again, there must be some good out there somewhere. So I'll cool it and save it for another day. I think you know the rest. You too read the papers and watch the news, so I'll not belabor the situation. My biggest concern is that our younger generation, those close to the voting age and many beyond, are not accepting this situation as something that cannot be resolved. Simply going to the voting booth won't do it. Substituting the players doesn't change the team. Leaders are made—not born. It is time to move the team and change the game plan. We need honesty, integrity, character, and patriots. This is our country, not theirs. Let's take it back.

AMERICA STILL THE GREATEST

MY NEGATIVE VIEWPOINT ON POLITICS practiced in this country may have created the impression that I'm not a happy warrior. This was not my intention. My inherited spirit of old-fashioned Americanism tells me that we live in the greatest country in the world with the greatest system of democracy ever designed for its people. And I'll pick up the gun once again in its defense should the need arise.

The problem lies in the abuse of every privilege allotted us to suit our own personal satisfaction and advantage. From a simple traffic regulation, where the rules call for a speed limit of sixty miles per hour on the highway, we'll do sixty-five because we think we can get away with it.

If your tax return allows a certain percentage deduction for chartable contribution, we'll take the max even though we never donated a dime to any charity. That's called taking advantage. Nevertheless, this is just the tip of the berg. It's the big stuff that counts.

And the big stuff is in Washington where the temptation is greatest. "Who knows what lurks in the hearts of evil men?" Some old-timers might remember that from the old radio series called *The Shadow*. If the abuse and deception is already in place, why not join the party? Or be left behind. We elect and send to Washington who we believe to be the best representatives to lead this country to bigger and better things for all people, not for themselves. It is not a free ticket, as indicative of the way Congress votes itself, to the exorbitant salaries, bonuses, useless political junkets, parties, and exemptions not available to the common citizen.

We have those infamous earmarks or porks—call them whatever you like. It's where billions of our tax dollars go for boondoggle projects to suit some politician's selfish interest—a system desperately in need of reform.

Welfare programs, designed for the unfortunate and the poor, are laced with fraud. Food stamp programs for the hungry are laced with fraud. The electoral voting system, voter registration, rules, and regulations set in place for us to select the best representatives are also laced with fraud.

Travel junkets all over the globe by politicians with their family and friends are at government expense. Why think of deficits and spending while casually sipping a Bloody Mary and soaking in a hot tub? Is this not fraud?

Even the traditional fundraisers, which we have for years supported one another with for whatever reason, are all laced with fraud. Just the size of the salaries for executive administrators should raise a red flag—a $400,000 salary and bonus that is annual to the head of a veterans fundraiser, a $675,000 paycheck paid annually for the executive of United Way, and a $951,000 paycheck paid to the American Red Cross administrator. The CEO of UNICEF receives a $1,900,000 salary plus expenses and the use of a luxurious vehicle. These fat cats all living high on the hog on your dollars.

Focus your attention on the unethical behavior in the corporate world. Industry giants like Enron—accounting fraud; Fannie Mae—underreporting profits but reaping huge bonuses; Halliburton—politically connected executives, overcharging government; and Tyco Corporation—well-publicized executive theft. Is there no end to this list of white-collar crooks?

Gone unnoticed but very real is the fraud in the pristine banking business with executives siphoning off millions from their own banks and depositors making false loan applications.

Let us not forget the medical professionals where we find massive medical fraud, particularly those billing practices in the Medicare program. The huge overcharging by hospitals and medical professionals so easy to beat in a program out of control . . . "How sweet it is."

Still more not to be passed over, it's our friends in the national labor unions. Despite extensive criminal investigations and being closely watched by the federal government, racketeering by organized crime is still prevalent and on the rise.

As I conclude my lament on the illicit workings of the government, once again, I say the system is OK! It's the loopholes that need plugging. And so we return to the voting booth; we make some titular changes, but the system remains the same. There will remain two senators representing your state, and you will continue to have a district congressman. Let them know you mean business. You send them your message. I'll send them this book. God bless America. You are the greatest.